Hearts Full of Compassion

Inspirations in the lives of ordinary women

Stories by
The Sisters of the Living Word

Edited and collected by
Nancy Burgess

"Woman's Song of Peace" copyright 1995 by Mary
Southard, CSJ. Published by the Ministry of the Arts,
Sisters of St. Joseph, LaGrange - Catalog: 800-354-3504
reprinted with permission from:
Ministry of the Arts
Sisters of St. Joseph, LaGrange
1515 W. Ogden Ave
LaGrange Park, Illinois
(800)354-3504

Stories contributed by:
The Sisters of the Living Word c/o
800 North Fernandez Avenue-B
Arlington Heights, IL 60004-5316
ph:(847)577-5972
Fax:(847)577-5980
e-mail address: slw@slw.org
website: www.slw.org

Published by Save-A-Barn Small Press,
Long Grove, IL 60047
Copyright 1999 Nancy Burgess
Cover Photo copyright 1999 Nancy Burgess

First published in the United States of America in 1999 by
Save-A-Barn Small Press, 5603 RFD
Long Grove, IL 60047
website: www.nsn.org/eakhome/savebarn
ISBN number: 0-9668749-1-9

Special thanks to the following people without whose help this book would not have been completed: the Sisters who donated their stories, Marie Roth for her editorial input, Rhoda Martin for believing in me and my dreams, my husband for supporting the many projects that I undertake, and my children for reminding me to take some time off every once in a while.

-N.B.

Dedication

To all who inspire us to compassion
S.L.W.

To all the women who need inspiration
This book is for them
N.B.

Contents

Introduction...1
The Sisters of the Living Word..................................5

Hearts Full of Compassion 9
Song of Peace 19
Song of Life's Seasons 29
Rhythms of Birth and Death.......................................33
Receiving and Giving 37
Times of Waiting and Fulfillment..........................45
Suffering and Joy...53
Listening and Hope..63
Wholeness and Unity...69
Harmony with Earth 77
Reverence for Earth's Gifts 81
Her Song is Compassion 85
Her Song is Love..89

Editor's Note...93
Journal Pages 95
Index to Sisters..129
Information...131

Introduction

"God created her; woman. And God gave her...a heart full of compassion..."*

I met the Sisters of the Living Word through a friend who served on their development board and knew that I was interested in women's issues. She told me that I had to meet these remarkable women.

As a lay person, not connected to the Catholic Church, I was a little intimidated meeting the Sisters initially. I expected stodgy, quiet, nun-like women. What I encountered were strong, gentle women, full of laughter and humility. When we talked at length about their lives, we realized that all had similar goals.

For myself, my goals are to help women focus their energies, and enable them to see their paths stretching before them with hope. For the Sisters, their goal is to teach women and men that God works mysteriously and blessedly in all our lives. Their deeds and actions are their way of showing how God is at work.

I learned, after talking to the Sisters, that even as they chose to give their lives to God, they still struggle with the same inner turmoil that we are all plagued with, the search for peace, and questioning whether the path they chose for their lives was the correct one. For the Sisters, this question is answered by those people whom they serve.

These common interests convinced us to merge our energy and resources and create this collection of stories. The Sisters were asked to send me stories about how simple

*from a poem entitled Woman that hangs in the lobby of the Sisters of the Living Word center in Arlington Heights, Illinois.

acts of kindness became moments of spiritual connection. These stories were not to be religious experiences, per se, but subtle signs from God above.

Reading these stories from the Sisters caused me to notice moments in my own life when I was lifted from the monotony of day-to-day living and reminded of the spirit around me. One such moment came while I was working on many projects and expecting a payment to arrive from one of these projects. I kept searching the mail and finally discovered a letter of unknown origin that I felt sure was the one I was anticipating. I opened the letter, and I must confess, was disappointed to see it was from one of the Sisters.

As I read the letter from Sister Mary Nicholas about how she stopped in her daily routine to help a stranger and how she was rewarded, I was humbled by my own lack of awareness of those in need around me. I was spending far too much time worrying about business and far too little time appreciating the gifts before me. In my hasty reaction to the letter, I had almost missed the blessing of the story from Sister Mary Nicholas.

I received many stories over the next several months, and each time I opened one of their letters I was amazed at the diversity of the Sister's reach. Simultaneously, I became much more aware of inspirational moments in my own life.

One particular evening stands out in my memory. I was driving into Chicago to attend an opera and meet with an old friend. Before leaving the house, I grabbed a few dollars to pay for parking and a cup of coffee during the show. I had $42 dollars total, two twenties and two ones.

When I exited the ramp into the city there was a woman standing next to a car signaling for help. Other automobiles were passing her by, and I debated whether I should pass her too. (I have tried to adopt a policy about this. I have vowed to myself not to turn away from a person in need.) I slowed down and lowered my window partially to hear what she was asking.

"Please ma'am?" she implored, with her arms raised in a defensive gesture. "I mean you no harm. We ran out of gas and need help to get my family home to Indiana."

I reached into my purse and grabbed the nearest bill to hand to her. As I lifted the bill to the window I winced a little seeing that it was one of the $20 bills, but I handed it to her anyway.

"Bless you," she said. "If you give me your address I will send it back to you."

"Not necessary," I replied, and I drove on to my destination.

I parked the car and handed the attendant my other twenty dollar bill to pay the $8 required for parking. As I put the change back into my purse, there, in my wallet was another $20 bill.

Skeptics who heard this story said I must have been mistaken about how much I had really brought with me, but the Sisters all nodded their heads, and said, "ah, yes, the loaves of bread."

Moments of such consequence I call inspiring because they are marked by the ability to feel peace and inner understanding. Inspiring moments are the times when we feel closest to God.

Our hope is that these stories will cause each reader to find and appreciate their own inspiring moments. Within each of us is the spirit of God, the beauty and the compassion that is our gift. Hearts full of compassion.....

-Nancy Burgess 1999

The Sisters of the Living Word

The Sisters of the Living Word are members of a new Congregation of women religious. In their efforts at renewal and adaptation of religious life after Vatican Council II, the Sisters came to realize that their vision, their hopes for ministry and personal development, and their desire to influence decisions were taking them in a new direction. Under the leadership of Sister Annamarie Cook, former Provincial Superior, in 1975 ninety sisters made the decision to leave the traditional congregation and be part of a new community. They serve in a diversity of pastoral and social service ministries in ten states and fifteen diocese in the South and Midwest.

The Sisters of the Living Word accept the challenge to work for human rights and dignity of each person whenever they may minister. They are a pro-active group of leaders who derive satisfaction from mentoring, enabling the gifts and talents of others, and improving the lives of those they serve. This is how they live their vision statement:

Rooted in the Word we are impelled to be God's language, transforming the world as we lean into life's unfolding revelation. We advocate passionately for the voiceless, risking uncharted paths. We listen in contemplative silence, attending to the call of simplicity and presence. We weave a network of connections among diverse peoples and in dissonant situations.

From the Appalachian Mountains to the United States-Mexican border and from the suburbs of Chicago to central Florida the community of seventy-nine sisters brings the

Living Word to those in need. The sisters are supported through their stipends and salaries for ministry and donations. This income supports them by paying their education, health care, rent, groceries, and basic needs.

The following stories are told by the sisters from experience in their respective ministries.* The stories of grief, hope, and humor describe how much the sisters receive and how much they learn and grow in faith and love in their service of others. Each lifetime is made up of inspiring moments of courage, strength, and gentleness. This collection affords an opportunity to be attentive to and to appreciate those moments.

---

* The names of those ministered to have been changed to respect the privacy of those individuals.

Woman's Song of Peace

The song of peace is a Woman's song:

She sings the song of life's seasons-
rhythms of birth and death, receiving and giving,
times of waiting and fulfillment, suffering and joy.

She sings a gentle song of listening and hope,
of wholeness and unity,
of harmony with earth
and reverence for earth's gifts.
Her song is compassion,
her song is love.

If nations would be healed,
woman's song must be sung.
If there would be peace,
woman's song must be heard.

Hearts Full of Compassion

Sister Kristine Vorenkamp works at a birthing center on the Mexico/United States border in a small town called Westlaco. Westlaco is a fertile agricultural area also known as the Rio Grande Valley. The Holy Family Birth Center is a compound of bright yellow buildings including a clinic, birthing rooms, and staff houses. It is a unique mission providing a safe and personal setting for natural childbirth to indigent families, mostly farm laborers and the unemployed. Some of these people are recent immigrants trying to find work to survive, but most have been here for years. They live in colonias, neighborhoods surrounded by agricultural fields. In recent years there have been improvements, but many still do not have water and sufficient sewage treatment. The housing at times provides barely enough shelter from the extreme heat of the summer and the short but very cold spells of winter. These families suffer from long bouts of unemployment, resulting in poor nutrition, and the instability that comes from having to make frequent moves as they migrate for work. Yet, though financially poor, they have many riches to share with the people who work at the Holy Family Birth Center, primarily family values and faith which Sister Kris says sometimes exceeds her own. Sister Kris came to work here because she had three goals; to become fluent in Spanish, to serve the poor, and to work in a community.

-N.B.

I have been told before that I have a gentle presence that is healing for others. I have learned from my past mistakes of not listening, or being judged unfairly myself, that to listen attentively to another is a great gift. Enabling others to speak their WORD, understand their WORD, and allow their WORD to live is a great gift.

There were times when I wondered what my purpose was here. I have a hard time easily jumping into conversations with the others who work here since my background is in education and pastoral ministry. Many young women, some new graduates, come to volunteer a year or less as staff nurses, or student nurse-midwives. Because I am neither a nurse nor a midwife, I feel at times outside of their circle of talk, their medical jargon and experience.

I have come to accept that, in terms of community, I was being called upon to support, listen, and enjoy the people here, rather than be an active participant in the medical process. This really was pointed out to me during my first Christmas here on the border.

That Christmas was not a typical day here except for the rainy cold of the weather. In the afternoon one of our 16- year-old mothers delivered a still-born. Gabby, a student midwife had gone to the hospital with the teen mother. We had all known that the baby would be stillborn, but the doctor wanted the mother to deliver the baby naturally.

Our staff had gathered for a delightful Christmas dinner where each of us was going to share a Christmas story, tradition or food. As we ruminated about the day we discussed the still-born baby and the birth of twins born earlier that day to one of our older mothers.

Gabby returned from the hospital, and as she began to relate how things went, about how the dead baby looked, and how tragic it was, the tears began to spill.

Gabby was weak from the experience. She and I went out to walk and talk, and grieve together. I listened to her pour out her heart and I felt the pain of Gabby and the young mother. On that Christmas we experienced both great joy and great pain. God had blessed us with the spectrum of life.

Gabby has visited our Center a few times since that year, and she always takes a moment to thank me for being there for her. Other nurses have also thanked me for my gentle presence and have said that it was a very important gift to them to have me here. I thank God for being able to learn to live in the Spirit and to allow others to come to know the WORD of God living in them.

At our birth center in the Rio Grande Valley of Texas, many of our clients live in outlying 'colonias' (neighborhoods on tracts of land amidst agricultural fields) and have no means of transportation except perhaps one run down car that may serve an extended family. So...we offer a taxi service for our prenatal visits, funded by grants, to bring the women into the clinic.

As it often went, one Wednesday evening I closed the front office and went for the car keys hanging in the kitchen. I was very hungry so I grabbed a banana and a small apple because I had a couple of hours on the road ahead of me. It was already 9 pm. I remember this night in particular, not for any great event that would happen, but for the simple gift the night would bring.

I was to take the women home that early evening, Maria, a vivacious 15-year-old, Ana, a delightful Honduran refugee, and Lidia, a working mom with four children and one on the way. Lidia's youngest, Alexa was also with us. All of these women were very poor, never knowing when the next meal would be, or how they would feed their children. They were trying to improve their lives, and do the best they could for their children. They were each in some step of the documentation process and constantly feared the threat of deportation. I was amazed at their ability to always be happy and full of fun.

Maria suggested that we go all the way to the farthest colonia first because Lidia was exhausted, and Alexa was antsy. On the way, the baby fussed and cried, and I tried a few tricks but they did not work. Finally, Maria, concerned, said to Lidia, "Tiene hambre?" *Is she hungry?*. Lidia said, "Si".

I thought to myself, "Kris, you forget that these women go hungry a lot, you dummy!" In fact, our resident nurse said just the other night that Lidia's ketones were so high that her baby within was very hungry too. So, impressed with Maria's sensitivity, and humbled by my lack of it, I gave Lidia my banana, which she gave to her daughter, and then the baby was content.

When we arrived at Lidia's trailita (*little trailer*), our sweet teen, Maria, very pregnant herself, jumped up, grabbed Alexa, and brought her into the trailer. I took in the box of food we had for them and we said good-bye.

We then headed for Maria's casita and as we began Maria said, "Yo tengo mucho hambre, tambien!" *I am very hungry, too.* I might have known that she was, if Ihad thought. I gave her my apple.

On the way, Maria realized that she was completely turned around in the dark and did not know how to tell me the way to her house. We had a good laugh, and I stopped to call the midwife on-call for directions. Then we were on our way.

After I dropped Maria off, I pondered my options of Whataburger or some pick of fruit at home and I was flood-ed with a wave of goodness. In the dark and quiet of the night I felt the same warmth that I always experience with our women. I was again pulled out of my comfortableness and overwhelmed by the blessings I receive from these women who struggle daily to survive.

These young women have husbands who are either not there, or gone north for work. These are people who are barely able to be who they want to be because of the poverty, and yet they still are sensitive to each other, and still find the joy in their lives. The power of new life that flows from them to us, no matter their circumstances, is a gift from God. It is also by God's grace that I can affirm it and be touched.

We, the living community of Sisters, volunteer R.N.s and nurse-midwives, grin and bear the thought of summer coming here in the Rio Grande Valley. I grew up in New Orleans in the days without air conditioning so I know what hot is. But, after my first summer here, I decided that no one living here will go to hell because they have it right here!

The community that lives on this mission chooses to live without air conditioning for two interrelated reasons; we cannot afford it, and we go without it in order that we can afford to have it in the clinic and birthing room to give the families a comfortable space to have their birth experience.

As we are only human, it can become very really unbearable. A favorite pastime here in the summer is to go to the movies or to the mall just to cool down. By September of this year we had just completed 60 straight days above 100 degrees. Sometimes the only way to survive something like that is by venting your frustrations.

One of our lunchtime conversations one day broke the heaviness of these dreadful days and added some levity as one of us said, "I have just returned from visiting my family and they were all crabbing about the heat! I just looked at them and said, 'you do not know what heat is until you cannot sleep at night and you soak your night gown with sweat so you can cool off!'"

Another said, "Hot is when you go to the bathroom, only you cannot even urinate because you have sweated all the liquid off."

Another chimed in, "Hot is when you can look forward to going UP (to heaven) because you already know you have been down (in hell) here!"

Finally, "You do not know hot until you have survived a summer in the Rio Grande Valley!"

We all laughed because it was all true!

Somehow, hanging in there together helps. I guess that is how the thousands of poor people, some who won't even buy a fan because it costs money to run, get by summer after summer in this incredible valley heat.

Life on the border continues to be tense. President Clinton says there will be no mass exportations, but in fact, they are happening at night. Busloads of laborers have been reported to be dropped off in Reynosa, across the border from McAllen. They seem to be rounding them up from Midwest factories and fields, and also from fields and flea markets here. The border cities in Mexico are being over-whelmed by it, we hear.

All of this affects those people we are trying to help. We decided as of Thanksgiving Day that God may be asking us to begin a 'no charge' policy. This decision is a result of our reflection on the effects that our patients are experiencing from the repeal of the Welfare and the new Immigration Laws. Our client base has been dwindling steadily. If we continue getting so few clients we would be forced to close.

We thought that perhaps our clients were leaving

because of the cost ($1200). Even though we charge far less than any doctor or hospital, it is still too much money for many of these women. If they could not pay before, we asked them to volunteer, but they were not available to do this. For some it was the cost of getting to the center, for others, they were not feeling well enough to volunteer. Still others were caring for elder family members or children from other families, and some of the women were working in the fields with their husbands.

Now we are telling the women that it still costs us $1200 for their care, but they can give whatever they want to help us. The amazing thing was that as soon as we decided that, the very day, in fact, we received a grant equaling $14,000 more than we had requested, and two other grants as well.

Suddenly, our caseload went up as well, back to normal. I believe that God desired an attitude change toward those who are greatly in need, and God provided the rest.

I continue to be grateful for my experience here and cherish the challenge of being present to people who live differently, many with great anxieties, and with few of the basic necessities, but who share great faith. It is amazing how many times these people have to move for so many reasons...and their daily lives are a struggle. They remind me of a Holy Family from 2,000 years ago. With their great faith and their determination, I believe that we will see our future leaders from some of these families.

Maria Valdez and I enjoyed our conversations ever since she first became a client at the Birth Center, and I worked at the reception desk. There was an immediate bond between us. Whenever she came for her check-ups we would find a moment to talk about her family, about the stresses and joys of her life, and her hopes for a healthy and safe pregnancy.

"Primeremente Dios" (God's Will first), she would always say.

I had not seen her in over a year when she called yesterday and shared her grief over the very recent death of her "suegra" mother-in-law. Maria's parents and children were in Mexico, her suegra was very dear to her, like another mother. She cried and shared the suffering that her suegra endured. Though they hoped and prayed for her to get well, in the end, her husband and cunadas, in-laws, decided to take her off the respirator.

I was very touched that Maria wanted to tell me, because I had not seen her in quite a while and I quickly realized that she was reaching out to someone she felt cared about her. I told her that I would visit her the next day.

As always happens, my efforts to reach out to another came back as a blessing. I arrived at Maria's trailita, as she was preparing tamales for the new year. I apologized and said that I forgot that this was a busy time.

"No importa", she said and we began our visit, she preparing the meat and I watching, as she would not let me help her. I did not push the issue, desiring to respect her hospitality.

Sitting there, I watched Maria preparing the food, in between breastfeeding the baby, tending to her 2-year-old, giving directions to her two older girls with loving patience, all the while talking to me about her life, her husband's struggles in the fields, her grief and dreams.

She told me how she had been divorced and had four children and her husband also had four children from another marriage. Her husband just last year got her papers completed for residency in the U.S. after years and payments of money to the government. Now, they will work toward residency for the Mexican-born children.

Maria had worked since she was 10, but somehow matured in love and devotion in her young life of 28 years.

There was never a note of bitterness or resentment, only gratitude. The love for her children, family and God, gently flowed from all of her actions.

She spoke of her hopes to learn to make galletas, cookies, but she did not yet have an oven only a stove top. All the while she spoke of how good God is and how God knows what we need.

I sat there listening in surroundings of simplicity that many would consider poverty, receiving the gift of this remarkable woman. Her love filled the insecurities of her life with hope, and blessed me with a light that filled my day. What a special way to spend this New Year's Eve a visit with a friend who generously sparkled peace to all around her. I feel certain that this gift will stay with me through this New Year.

Song of Peace

Since 1992, Sister Betty Betzwieser has been working as a tutor in a first grade setting. In 1996, she was asked to work as a teacher's aide for the 1st and 2nd grade Polish bilingual program at the same Chicago Public School. Prior to that time, she had spent 25 years as an elementary school teacher at various Catholic Schools and also ministered as a Director of Religious Education in two suburban parishes.

-N.B.

In the early 1990's, while in transition between ministries, I befriended a senior citizen, Marie, who was very lonely. She faced the challenges of adjusting to her new surroundings as she grieved over her husband's recent death.

One year, before Christmas Eve, this woman shared her story of the ups and downs in family relationships. The bottom line was that she felt forced to open gifts that she received from out-of-state family alone, even though she had family living a few miles away. She was visiting the local family on Christmas, but was told not to bring her gifts because the wrappings would be too messy.

We talked for some time and I offered to be with her for a few hours before joining my own family's celebration on Christmas Eve.

This lifted her spirits. My presence and entering into her joy of gift-opening eased her pain and was deeply appreciated.

It was such a small gesture on my part, and yet, I think of this when I consider all those that are alone or suffering during the holidays. Sometimes those small gestures make a big difference. Her Christmass now are celebrated with her Maker.

⊰⊱∞⊰⊱

Recently, I had a unique experience at the public school where I work. We had an assembly in the gym with all the Kindergarten through 3rd grade children, and their parents, about 700 in all.

Being from a Catholic background, these are always challenging experiences for me. They remind me of what the old census in ancient times must have been like, hundreds of people jammed into one room, so much noise and chaos. Could this have been what Joseph and Mary encountered when they returned to Bethlehem?

The children were putting on their programs, singing songs, and fidgeting from nerves and excitement. After our group performed, the first graders stepped up to sing their songs. The children with learning disabilities were grouped with the first graders and one boy in particular really caught my eye.

I had seen this boy often in the hallways. He was severely disabled. He always seemed so filled with tension and discomfort. Today, he was right in the middle of the first row of performers, as they began singing, "I saw Momma kissing Santa Claus".

For the time that the song was playing it was as if this child was no longer handicapped. In almost a trance, he lost himself in the music, creating his own gestures, singing and swaying to the rhythm. He was one with the spirit of the season, and his transformation lifted me to the same feeling of hope, and joy. The song ended and he was soon back to experiencing his insecurity and anxiety.

It was a brief experience. But, for a moment he was unconscious of who he was. We had both felt that release from the burdens of the chaos, the weight of the everyday stress of living had been taken away, and I felt that I had been truly blessed with a precious moment which lingers in my memory. I was reminded again of the magic of the season, the celebration that is Christmas.

Sister Jeannine Randolph taught grades first through twelfth in Catholic Schools for 21 years. Her teaching carried her from Chicago to the Bayou in Louisiana. She ended her teaching career at St. Margaret Mary in Algonquin, Illinois after 10 years there as the Pastoral Minister. Today, Sister Jeannine is training a Novice (a new Sister starting out). Sister Jeannine is also a certified Massage Therapist who brings the gift of massage therapy to local nursing centers.

-N.B.

W hen I was in the Bayou I met a wonderful Native American man, Father Frank, who was the priest at the parish where I was teaching. His story of how he came to be where he was has inspired me as I have ministered to people through the years.

As a young boy, Frank was very poor. He attended the local Indian school because Native Americans were not permitted to attend the white school. In sixth grade Frank told his mother that he wanted to be a priest. His mother took him to the local pastor, who told him to work hard in school and attend the seminary after high school, if he was still inclined.

When Frank got to eighth grade the school was so poor that they were using the books from seventh grade over again. Not wanting to repeat seventh grade, Frank took a year and went oystering in the ocean to earn money for his family. After a year of this his mother reminded him that if he was still serious about being a priest he would have to finish his education.

He returned home and High School was spent in Thibodaux, Louisiana where he finally learned about nouns and verbs.

He entered the seminary after high school and struggled terribly. Aside from failing every class, he suffered prejudice from the seminarians who gave him a can of 'ss' to mock him for not knowing where the 's' went in words. After the first year at the seminary he was called into the Dean's office and told that he would never make it. When he told his mother this, she sent him back and said, "We will pray you through this."

Frank went back, worked hard and retook the tests. Finally, he passed the classes. After the seminary he went to Arkansas to be ordained because he was told that he would never qualify in the Bayou.

When Frank returned, an ordained minister, he insisted on staying in the Bayou. After all that he had overcome, this was still his home.

Frank is one of the holiest priests that I have ever met. His Native American background gave him a special connection to the earth and nature and his way with people was something that I have tried to emulate through the years. He has always impressed me as a man who was 'good all the way down to the soul.' I remember him often as I go about my own ministries as a person who inspires and teaches the meaning of the word faith.

When I was working at St. Margaret Mary in Algonquin, Illinois I met a young mother, Theresa, through the RCIA program that I was directing. When we met she was pregnant with her first baby, Patrick. Our friendship remained as Patrick grew.

One day in the summer we were leaving a function at the church and commenting on how hot it was, and how hot the cars would be by now. Theresa had just put Patrick, who was now two years old, into his carseat in the van. She tossed her keys to the other side and closed the door. As Theresa closed the door, Patrick reached toward the door and pushed down the lock, which simultaneously locked all of the other doors. Patrick was locked in the car.

Theresa was frantic as she considered her options. Imagining the heat in the van, I looked in at Patrick, who started giggling when he saw me. "You try to get in, I will distract the baby," I said.

Theresa ran to the church and tried to solicit help, while I ran around the van, popping up, and yelling "Peek-a-boo!"

The liturgy coordinator came out with a hammer and tried to smash a window, but none would budge.

Theresa said, "I think I have some extra keys at home." she said, "It is not far, we can drive quickly while Sister Jeannine keeps playing."

"Go ahead," I said, as I ran from one side of the car to the other, still popping. It was amazing that Patrick was still smiling, barely noticing the rising temperature in the van.

They returned without the keys. By this time Theresa was near panic. She and the liturgy coordinator went into the church and called the local police.

Meanwhile, after about one half hour of watching me bounce around, the baby was getting a little tired of my games, and starting to feel the effects of the heat. When the police arrived, little Patrick had had enough. The police were able to jimmy the locks and release the baby.

Even though it has been several years, Theresa still reminds me of that day. She says that if I had not been there to keep Patrick calm, she is not sure what she would have done. In retrospect, I thank God for giving that baby the humor and patience that probably saved his life.

⋘∞⋙

While I was at St. Margaret Mary in Algonquin, Illinois

there was a mix-up in scheduling for one of our Saturday evening Masses and neither of our two priests showed up to conduct the mass. We tried to reach them both, but they were nowhere to be found.

I looked out into the sanctuary and there were 500 or 600 people there, waiting for mass to begin. The liturgist said to me, "everything is in place, what are we going to do?"

"We will have a communion service," I decided.

The music began. In came the cross bearer. In came the candle bearer. In came me dressed in a blue and white robe.

I went to the front of the altar and when I went to make the sign of the cross, out of my mouth came, "What do you think the Pope would say in this situation?" the audience clapped.

What could I do? I read the gospel, gave the homily (I was most concerned about this) started the prayers for the offering, and the liturgist whispered, "you forgot to collect the offering."

"I am sorry," I said, "I am not a priest, I forgot the offering." Everyone laughed.

There was no consecration of the host, but we conducted the communion. As the parish came up to receive their communion there were many comments, "Beautiful job, Sister!", "Oh, this is fine." , "This is just great," "We should do this more often."

When the benediction was over, the congregation started clapping. It was such an affirming service. We had all shared such a communion of faith.

That evening, I called the pastor at home and asked, "Where were you? There was no one to run the service." I said. "I had a communion service by myself."

He was surprised, but said, "That was just fine, Sister."

When I was a little girl, I attended Catholic school. Even though my father was not Catholic. When I was learning about being Catholic, and the importance of being Catholic, I would come home and ask my dad when he was going to become a Catholic. My mother said to stop talking about it with him. "He will do things in his own time," she explained.

I continued with the Catholic schools, and eventually became a nun. My father still never became a Catholic.

After I had taught for several years, my father had a stroke and went into the hospital. I came home to be with my mother and my father. As we were driving to the hospital my mother asked me, "Honey, why don't we call a priest to come and baptize dad."

"Oh Mom," I replied, "He is such a good man, the Lord will let him into heaven, he does not need to be a Catholic," This from his daughter the nun.

My mother was adamant, "We would have gotten him involved in the last few years, he wanted to learn, but we have been so busy taking care of his mother, that we lost track of time."

I still felt that he would be fine, but mother insisted on calling the priest when we got to the hospital. She got the priest on the phone, and asked him to come over. Then she added, "my daughter, the nun, does not think this is necessary," she paused for a moment and then handed the phone to me. "He wants to talk to you."

The priest said that we should leave it up to my dad, but that he would come over. "Ask your father," he suggested, "maybe he will tell you."

We entered my father's room. I looked at this shell of my dad lying on the bed, and asked him gently, "Dad? Do you want to be baptized now?"

He sat up in the bed, looked me in the eye, and clearly said, "Yes," before he collapsed back onto the mattress and

27

was incoherent again.

The priest came, baptized my father, and shortly thereafter my father passed away. All his life he spent taking care of us, and finally we were able to take care of him.

Song of Life's Seasons

Sister Marlene Geimer spent 21 years in education, 10 years as a teacher and 11 years as an administrator. For the past 10 years she has been working full-time as the treasurer for the Sisters of the Living Word in Arlington Heights. These stories are drawn from her time as an administrator with St. Gregory Elementary on the North side of Chicago. Sister Marlene worked there because she wanted to make a difference. St. Gregory's was a parish that was always in need of money, and yet, always seemed to have just enough. The Sisters suspected that the Pastor of the parish abstained from accepting a salary so that the church could stay afloat.

-N.B.

It was a brisk November day when Susan came to my office asking that I would not send her child home even though she was behind in tuition payments. She had a baby under two years of age in her arms while trying to explain that she was also supporting her mother who had cancer.

Her husband had left her and she was really strapped between trying to feed the family, and keeping her child in a Catholic school, where Susan felt her daughter would fare better than in the local public schools.

"I am in the midst of selling my baby's furniture," she explained, "I will have the money then."

"How have you been managing up to now?" I asked.

"I have been selling my furniture piece by piece" she replied.

I immediately went to the school board finance person and requested that the tuition be lowered or waived completely for Susan, which it was, and she was very grateful.

Later, I discovered that Susan still had $150 to pay for the birth of the baby. For close to two years she had, little by little, dwindled the balance.

I was planning to have a Christmas raffle for the children in the school. The money was raised to give to someone in need. Without letting Susan know that the money raised would be for her, I asked her what she would really like to give to her children for Christmas so that Santa Claus would bring the right things.

Never before and never since that Christmas Eve have I experienced such personal joy and joy of others. Around 11:00 pm after the children were in bed, I brought Santa's gifts for the children.

Some things Susan and I put together and placed by the tree. Others were already wrapped as a surprise for both mom and the children. In the bottom of Santa's sack was a little box for Susan.

"Here," I said, "it is a special gift for you."

I will never forget her eyes as they lit up not just because of all the excitement, but that there was a gift for her too.

Her mother sat next to her on the floor as she opened her little box. There were three 50 dollar bills rolled up and a message to pay the doctor's bill in full. Her mother cried, she cried and even Santa's helper cried.

I have lost touch with Susan over the years. But I know, and she knows that we will never be the same and there will never be another Christmas like that one.

While I was a principal at St. Gregory there was a tragic story about one of the students in the first grade class. The child's mother had been shot and killed in a bar where she worked.

When I went to the wake, I noticed the little girl was not present. I asked around and discovered that the grandparents had chosen not to tell the child. They told the girl that her mother had gone on a long trip and they did not know when she would return.

When I heard this I went a little crazy, something was compelling me to make these grandparents see their error. I called and pleaded with the grandparents. "This child can handle this, please do not lie to her. She needs this finality." The grandmother was firm in her decision.

I tried again. "Please," I pleaded, "please reconsider. A child who is not given a chance to say good-bye to her mother will spend her whole life searching and wondering where her mother went and why she left her. She needs to know that her mother is with God."

Finally, I had the parish priest call them. He, too, was unsuccessful. Again, I talked to the grandmother, and she finally said, "I cannot tell her how she died, it is just too tragic."

"You do not have to give her all the gory details, just tell her that she has died, and gone to live with God." I thought quickly, "Would it make you feel better if her teacher was there?"

"Yes, that would be good," the grandmother finally agreed. "We will tell her."

I frantically called the child's teacher, Sister Caroline, "Please come to the funeral home and help this little girl."

When the child arrived, she talked with Sister Caroline outside the viewing room for a while. The Sister explained how someone dies and then goes to live with God. Then, they went together to see her mother lying in the casket. The little girl touched her mother and said good-bye and then she sat in her teacher's arms on the floor by the casket and wept.

The following morning, the little girl was not at the

funeral, but she was with the family at the home. She heard some others talking about her mother dying and she said, "My mom is not dead!" Everyone held their breath in shocked silence before she added, "My mom is alive with God!"

After this event the family sent me chocolates, and thanked me profusely for helping them to see why they needed to include the daughter in the mourning process. My concern was only for the little girl. Children need to know that part of the whole circle of life is death. They are usually much more resilient and accepting than we give them credit for. Children's lives are shaped by our actions towards them when they are little. I was just glad to have stopped the grandparents from making a tragic error.

Being an administrator in a Catholic school sometimes means going beyond just the business of the school; it often means personally touching the lives of the children we are teaching.

Rhythms of Birth and Death

Sister Mary Ann Zrust started her career as a teacher and then moved on to various administrative positions in several Catholic schools. After serving on the Leadership Team for the Sisters of the Living Word, she found herself open for a new position. Today she is an Administrative Assistant at the Vicar for Priest's Office in the Chicago Archdiocese.

-N.B.

For 10 years I worked in Berwyn, Illinois at St. Mary of Celle Church. The parish was a wonderful mix of cultures sharing their faith. When I arrived they needed guidance to establish outreach programs, so I set up a Pastoral/Social Ministry program at the church to serve the needs of the poor, the grieving, and the sick. At this position I helped train the lay people to function as ministers to these needs.

The people we ministered to through the church in Berwyn helped confirm my reasons for becoming a nun. It was a good and fruitful relationship. What I received the most gratification from was being present to those in need. Many times the gratitude and response of those who were sick or grieving was the catalyst for something greater, like one incident that really stands out in my memory.

It was a Sunday evening in spring when I was called to attend the wake of a young man who had died. As the pastoral associate, I often attended the wakes of deceased parishioners. I was aware of the young man's death, but knew neither him nor the family. It is always uncertain how the family, particularly if you do not know them, will respond to one's presence.

I am only human and, at first I hesitated to abandon a relaxing Sunday evening, but something nudged me to make the twenty-minute trip to be present with the grieving family. Taking the time to extend kindness to others can help bring comfort at a time when they experience emptiness and loss.

When I walked into the funeral home I was faced with a father who was in uncontrollable grief. The father's son, John, had been in his mid-twenties. He was on his way home from military service in the navy when he was struck by a semi-truck and fatally injured.

John had survived a few days in a hospital hundreds of miles from home. His father and stepmother had traveled to be with him for his final hours of life.

The father sobbed in my arms unable to cope with the sorrow that had come into his life. I offered my presence to him and his family and comforted him as I best I could. As long as I was needed, I stayed with the family and helped them accept the grief they were experiencing.

Later, I learned that this grief and my being there was the beginning of the father's return to God. Worship and prayer again became part of his life because he found a caring faith community that embraced him in the time of his greatest sorrow.

From time to time I am reminded that when we pull ourselves away from our own comfort zones to be there for others we are rewarded. Such a simple act as being there for a grieving family can mean the difference between their peace with God or their anger.

God can call us more than once in our lives, and sometimes in different ways. When I was called to become a member of the Sisters of the Living Word it was a turning point for me. I realize now that that call prepared me for all the work that I have done since then.

Our mission to reflect and affirm the WORD of God has enabled me to be more accepting of my purpose. By our very title we are able to carry forth life. Life has happened for me because I have strived to live the WORD. This has been pointed out to me most recently in the way that I acquired my current ministry.

I was cleaning out my office because my term on the leadership team of the Sisters of the Living Word was coming to an end. I was going to take a little time off and decide where I would go to minister next on this faith journey.

At the same time, unbeknownst to me, the Vicar for the Priest's Office in the city of Chicago was looking for someone to work in their office. They had been searching for 8 or 9 months for someone to fill the position and contacted a friend of mine. Did she know anyone in her religious community who might be interested?

My friend said that she did not, but suggested that perhaps I would consider the position. Within 20 minutes the Priests had contacted me and called me down for an interview.

I arrived at their office at the appointed time, and on the way I felt this strong movement within myself to take the position. This was an opportunity that could not be passed. Sometimes all the actions of the universe fall into place and we realize that this is the path clearly leading us forward.

My previous experiences hold me in good stead. I am applying my skills and gifts to bring a new perspective to this ministry. While on the surface the position is clerical, I find that my skills enhance the job and allow me to minister to the Priests of the Archdiocese of Chicago.

God does work in mysterious ways. One day it may seem like the road before you is full of uncertainty, and in a matter of moments the call can come and the path leads to a clearer purpose. I have always found that when I accept God's plan for me, I am rewarded in surprising and wonderful ways.

Receiving and Giving

*Sister Joanne Fedewa has spent the last 10 years
as Pastoral Coordinator at Christ the King Church in
Flint, Michigan. The Pastoral Coordinator manages the
day-to-day operations of the Church. There is no priest
in residence. Each week-end a visiting priest conducts the
masses, almost like the traveling ministers of old. Prior to
this work, Sister Joanne held the position of Principal,
Director of Religious Education, served on theLeadership
Team of the Sisters of the Living Word, and was a teacher
for many years, teaching in many schools throughout
the country.*

-N.B.

"How beautiful on the mountain top are the feet of the one
who brings tidings of peace, joy and salvation." Is.52

This passage has always impressed me and has urged
me to live the passage as I go about my ministry.
This passage was with me as I went to minister to
women inmates on Wednesday evenings at our County Jail.

I had never done this kind of work before. I had been a
teacher for years before moving to Flint, Michigan to be the
Pastoral Coordinator of Christ the King Church.
Ministering to the women inmates was part of the outreach
program I began.

Imagine my fear, entering the jail through one security
door after another. I really did not know what to expect
when I finally got to meet these women. The heavy doors
kept closing behind me, trapping me in a new chamber,
before the next would open as we went deeper and deeper
into the jail.

Finally, I came to the area where the women were waiting, and there before us were women who were eager and open to speak to me. My fears vanished as I met these beautiful women trapped in lives where they had little control.

The women were there for various reasons. Some were there because they stole to feed their families after their husbands left. Some had written bad checks and others had suffered from drug or alcohol abuse. None of them was violent.

The women seem to really enjoy the visits. We read scriptures, pray together, and have discussions about what the scripture passages mean. They tell me how much they want to change their lives, and how touched they are by my reaching out to them.

We are beginning to create a follow-up program to continue to help these women when they leave jail. They have only known one way to live, and the reality of world on the outside is so different for them. Many return to prison. I get letters from some of them telling me how they are doing. One day I was stopped by a woman on the street who recognized me from the prison and thanked me for being there for her.

It has been remarkable, how I have changed my own feelings from that first time when I entered that jail. That day I was feeling we were bringing something to them, but on departing each visit, I rejoice in the love and deep appreciation that I receive from these women. I have come to recognize in them their deep goodness and their desire to live better lives. Whenever I leave, I do so feeling that the rewards were equal. They, too, are on the mountaintop with us, bringing us good news.

⋘⋙

Being in the right place at the right time is often how

God works miracles to lift up his people. Such was the case one day when the rectory doorbell rang. Upon answering, I found a total stranger weeping and asking if she could come in to speak to me. I hesitated before saying yes, because I was alone and my parishioners never want me to permit strangers to visit with me when I am alone. But I dared and trusted God to be with me, and God was with me.

A depressed and devastated woman poured out her story. She, who had lived her marriage vows faithfully for 32 years, found out that her husband had been unfaithful to her, and a son had been born of this unfaithfulness. What pain filled her heart. The office was filled with her cries of anguish. I listened. I cried with her. I was present for her. Together, we talked and prayed for healing and strength. Finally, I told her to come back whenever she wished.

Time has helped to heal her wounds. Today, she is separated from her husband, but still faithful. I admire her willingness to go on with her life. She continues her work, and her faith in God grows stronger every day.

She has returned many times and continues to tell me how she has been lifted up through our visits of sharing and prayer. I thank God for the courage to open the door to a stranger, and welcome her in as a friend, and a friend she is indeed.

There is a kind gentleman in our parish who surprised me greatly a few years ago. He is a married, family man who is a well respected member of the community. When he learned that we were ministering to the local jail, he took it upon himself to order a dozen bibles for us to take and give to the inmates.

Imagine the women's great surprise to not only read the bible with us, but also to have their own bibles to study during the week when we were not there.

It is hard to determine the impact this has had on these women inmates. This is the only time in their lives that they have been educated in Christianity.

It is easy to take for granted an upbringing that included attending church. For many, the catechisms or Sunday school were a natural part of a traditional Christian home. For most of these women, this is all new. Holding the gift of a bible in one's hand is like opening a door to hope.

This man has purchased bibles many times over the years, always without any initiation on my part. More recently he has added small devotionals to give as gifts also. I am grateful for the blessing this man has brought to these women, and grateful that I can be the instrument through which the gift is delivered.

"Train up a child in the way she should go, and when he is old, she will not depart from it." *Proverbs 22:6*

There is a little girl named Mercedes who visits our parish regularly with her grandparents. She is a real pleasure to encounter.

Both of Mercedes' parents work at full-time careers. Her grandmother spends a great deal of time with her because of her parents' working, and because her grandmother enjoys her company so much, and always has.

When Mercedes was three years old, she had heard the hymn, "Standing in the need of prayer." The hymn goes something like this: "Not the preacher, not the deacon, not the teacher, O Lord, But, me I am standing in the need of prayer."

Some days after hearing this hymn, her grandmother couldn't find Mercedes. She called for her, "Mercedes, what are you doing?"

"I am here, Grandma," she said standing still in the middle of the room, "I am standing in the need of prayer."

This past holiday, Mercedes, now six, was honored to be able to say the Christmas grace for the family. She read from her grandfather's prayer book and proudly said the blessing as her family gathered together to celebrate the feast and the birth of our Lord.

Children such as Mercedes give me hope for the future generation. These are the children that will leave behind this ghetto, and rise above oppression through their good works and their strong faith. These are the families that fill my life with untold blessings. It is an honor to be a part of this world.

Sister Phoebe Marshall has been a teacher for over 30 years. Her teaching career was spent in various Catholic schools around the nation. Some time was spent in Minneapolis, New Orleans, Chicago, and St. Louis. This story is from her experience in St. Louis.

-N.B.

There are some relationships that are my reason for doing the work that I do. While I was teaching in St. Louis, I spent time working with the GED program tutoring adults who wanted to continue their education. I was always impressed with the ambition of the people in this program. They so wanted to improve their lives, and such was the case with Rhonda.

Rhonda lived in the toughest project in St. Louis, the Pruitt-Igoe homes. This project was eventually destroyed. In fact, because of its reputation, there was national attention when it was pulled down.

Every Sunday afternoon I went to see Rhonda at her home for extra tutoring. Others were nervous for my going into the Pruitt-Igoe homes, but I had no fear, God was protecting me. The cockroaches on the walls, the graffiti telling of gang turf wars, and the noises resonating through the building, seemed to fade when I got to Rhonda's door.

Our time together was precious. Rhonda had dreams of becoming a nurse, and she was working hard to improve her life for herself and her family. I would have walked through a war zone to help her.

When Rhonda received her degree, she wrote that I was the best friend she had ever had. She is a nurse today, doing what she dreamed of doing. I cling to her words of friendship. This is a treasure of my life with God, helping others.

Times of Waiting and Fulfillment

Sister Judiann Derhake has been teaching in Gretna, Louisiana for 23 years. She received her Montessori training in Milwaukee, Wisconsin and taught in Wilmette, Illinois before she came to Gretna. She and Sister Jeannette teach the preschool 3, 4 and kindergarten Montessori program together at St. Anthony's School. Their team approach to teaching works well with the little ones, and they feel that staying where they are has been what God has intended for them.

-N.B.

After teaching 23 years in the same place, you get to see the children grow into adulthood. When you are with these little children, you can sometimes envision what they will be like when they are older. It has been wonderful to see how they have turned out, although we have lost track of some.

One of the boys I had in the preschool three program was Jonathan. Upon graduating from high school and before entering West Point, he was to pick a teacher who made a difference in his life. He chose me and put me in Who's Who in America's Teachers.

I was absolutely stunned by this. I mean, there had been plenty of other teachers in his 12 years of schooling, and I was just his pre-school teacher. When I reflect back on Jonathan, I remember a child who was always pleasant to be around, a nice little guy. He sent me a letter before entering my name and told me that I was someone who really stuck out in his mind when he thought back on teachers.

It was pretty awesome to be remembered in such a kindly, complimentary manner.

We are on the Parish Social Ministry committee and we help coordinate the Thanksgiving and gift food baskets and Christmas gifts for needy families in the area. This year we helped put together over 100 baskets at Thanksgiving and around 85 for Christmas. What impresses me the most about this project is not just the act of doing something for the people who need the help, but the way that the community of our church joins together to get the job done.

Usually, the Pastor announces that help is needed and we never cease to be amazed at the variety of help that arrives. This past year we had over 150 volunteers that came to put corn and beans and food packages together. Some of the folks were elderly members of the community, who felt that this was their duty to come and help, even when they could not lift things and had trouble walking. A great portion of the youth of our church come together, on their own, to help out along with new members of the congregation who offer their time and/or their vehicles to help deliver.

The most amazing people who help are those families that have been helped in the past, who are now back on their feet, and who have come to give back what they had received.

Events like this are so unifying, and give us such hope. Groups of people joining together to help one another are the cornerstones of community, and another way that God shows us he is indeed at work in our lives.

Sister Jeannette Daniel taught first grade in Morton Grove, Illinois at St. Martha's, and St. Theresa's in Chicago for 13 years before she came to Louisiana. She has been teaching with Sister Judiann in Gretna, Louisianna for 22 years.

-N.B.

Teaching God's little children is our life. We love to watch these youngsters grow, and we appreciate our opportunities to help their parents cope.

There was a little boy named Mario who was brought to school every day by his father. It took a few weeks before the little Mario was comfortable with the separation from his dad. The first day that Mario was dropped off at the school he was happy and social until he realized that his father had gone, then he proceeded to run out of the building after his father. I tried to keep him out of the street, and he pulled off my glasses and struggled to get away, all the while screaming for his dad. His father did see him and came back to help him adjust as he explained that the boy's mother had left the family when he was an infant.

Mario's father tried very hard to raise his son properly, but he was hindered by his own inability to read. It took us a while to realize why Mario was not doing homework, or why his father had missed meetings, but when we did realize the problem, we attempted to help his dad.

We found that we could help this father by calling him into the class room and making sure that upcoming events were told to him. We worked on flashcard words with him, and gave him some of the elementary primers. After a time, Mario's dad was able to write his own name rather than just signing an X.

Unfortunately, when Mario was ready for the first grade,

his mother decided to come back and she sued for custody, and won. We grieved with Mario's father for his loss; he had worked so hard to do the right thing for his son.

Teaching has its challenges, and its rewards. We have been blessed to share in the growth of these children of God, to see their achievements, and to share in their lives. For this we are grateful.

There was a Vietnamese family that lived across the street from our school in some pretty run down apartments. The children attended St. Anthony's School and they did not know very much English.

After school, we would help these kids read their homework assignments and complete their work in our classroom until their Mom would come to pick them up. Sometimes we would walk them across the street when they knew she would be home from work.

One Saturday, we were working in our garden next to our classroom. We were planting string beans and the kids came over eating white rice with chop sticks. They wanted to know what we were doing and so we showed them the bean seeds and explained how we were planting the seeds to grow bean plants.

We, in turn, asked the children what they were eating and they told us that it was Vietnamese food.

These were smart kids, and they did not need our help for a very long time. Today, two of the kids are in high school and two have gone to college. The two youngest received scholarships from our school so that they could attend the high school and they hope to be doctors when they grow up.

As a thank you for our help, their father, who is a shrimper, brings us shrimp every once in a while. It is a sweet relationship. Just one of the many reasons that we love our work here in Gretna.

*Sister Annamarie Cook is the founder of the Sisters of
the Living Word. She said that she helped found this
order because she saw a lot of Sisters who were unhappy
with the way that things were being run in the group they
were formerly connected to. Many of the younger Sisters
were leaving because they were so unhappy. By forming
this order, which required permission from the original
order, the Archdiocese and the Pope himself, Sister
Annamarie solved the problem. The first step to positive
change is recognizing that a change needs to be made.
It took a lot of courage for Sister Annamarie to make those
first steps and to have the vision to see beyond the problems that would be encountered in order to make
the change. A quiet, modest woman, Sister Annamarie
sees life in her own unique way.*

-N.B.

I met God today on the bus on my way to Golf Mill.
Outwardly it did not seem like God, in whatever way I
think God should be. However, it was God sitting next
to me on the bus. She began to relate her problems.
Especially she told how much drugs were rampant in her
area. I did not get everything she said because I will be
needing hearing aids soon, but I kept nodding my head in
sympathy with her and she was satisfied.

However, God had exceedingly bad breath and I kept
wishing that I knew her sufficiently well to be able to tell
her how to get rid of it. As it was, I quietly listened and nodded until she left the bus at a stop earlier than my own.

I keep on watching for God all the time, because sometimes it is difficult to see him/her. God is easier to find in
nature. I really would like to know....have you met God
today?

⋖⋗∞⋖⋗

Awhile back, I had a very awesome experience. I had left the bus in order to stop at the Jewel food store and pick up a few items that we needed. Coming out of the store, I joined another woman who was waiting for the same bus that I was hoping to board. Meantime, we sat on the bench and talked. She told me enthusiastically about the wonderful bargain that she had found at Jewel. Fresh raisin bread was on sale and she had bought two loaves.

Reaching into her bag, she drew out one loaf of bread and proceeded to open the package. She drew out a slice which she handed to me. She drew out another slice for herself, and there we sat munching the bread as we waited for the bus. For me, it was a profound experience of communion. Aren't we all ONE in the Spirit?

Suffering and Joy

Sister Mary Nicholas has tried to work where Catholic teachers are desperately needed. She has been teaching for 42 years. These stories are from her time at St. Raphael's parish in Chicago, where she taught for 13 years, her time in Canton, Mississippi, where she spent 5 years and from her most recent time in New Orleans, Louisiana where she has been teaching 5th grade for the last 18 months.

-N.B.

While biking in Canton, Mississippi, I became accustomed to biking past an old rambling shack in a lovely oak tree setting. The shack was falling to pieces among other upscale homes. It was nestled in a small patch of oaks seeming to be waiting for a stiff wind to knock it over.

One warm Saturday morning I was biking past, as usual, when I noticed someone sitting outside of this hut. She was a tall, thin, elderly woman. Her right arm was paralyzed and kept close to her body. My bike seemed to automatically steer in her direction.

Without saying even a hello, I asked in alarm, "Do you live here?"

"Yes," she replied proudly, "and I pay $40 a month rent."

We talked for a while, I discovered her name was Lillian. I was stunned that someone actually lived in this hut which I felt sure was abandoned. She told me she had children who occasionally stopped to visit. By the time I parted, fire filled my veins, that someone could live in such deplorable conditions!

I immediately contacted the city hall, and found the landlord. As I worked on this I made it part of my schedule to stop and chat with her.

During my next visit, Lillian invited me inside. I hesitated doing this, because through the door I could see the large floor holes, open invitations to snakes and....I could have cried in disbelief! There were boards sticking up in places, a stove sat in the middle of the floor and a single bulb hung from a cord casting the only light.

When prodded, Lillian explained that when the weather got cold, she would put cardboard on the windows and huddle in a sort of nest in one corner for warmth. She did have a TV to keep herself company.

Lillian felt helpless about changing her plight. She was a proud woman who was not unhappy. She was reluctant to fight for better housing when she could support herself comfortably on her government check, although her children sometimes asked her for some portion of the check.

We shared God's words and discussed her future and her conditions with her landlord. Finally, she agreed to be moved to a housing project where she has settled nicely.

Whenever I am in Canton, I still visit with Lillian. She has the same old cooking utensils ("why get new when the old work just fine", she says). She feeds me with her strong faith and her ability to feel secure amid so much poverty.

Upon reflection, I realize that even 'biking' leads to unchartered paths in my life.

As a teacher I find that it is really important to make teaching fun and to have a good time with the kids. Humor is a part of everyday. Some things are truly silly, like having the kids repeat exactly what I say. Recently I asked the class: What is an island? I had one boy repeat after me, "an island is an area of land surrounded by milk," He repeated the statement and then realized the mistake and burst into laughter with the rest of the class.

Sometimes I forget to tell the kids that I am just joking around. When I was teaching at St. Raphael on the south side of Chicago many years ago there was a particularly funny occasion. Those were the years when we wore habits and the kids were really curious about what we really looked like, and what our baptismal names had been.

I was teaching a group of remedial kids and they had really been bugging me about my name, so I spent a great deal of time telling them how embarrassed I was about the name, and how I could not wait to change it. I explained that I had been born with a long nose, and my parent noticed this immediately and wanted to name me appropriately. The children were crazy with curiosity, "what was it Sister Mary Nick, what....?"

Finally, I told them, "Pinocchio". Their eyes grew wide, and they covered their mouths to stop from laughing. The class ended quickly and they filed out spilling into the hallway with bursts of laughter.

1 month later, I realized that I had forgotten to take the story back, when a mother came in to have a conference. After discussing her child's progress, the mother became very serious. "Sister", she said, "I must ask you a very personal question."

"Go right ahead," I replied.

"Was your baptismal name really Pinocchio?"

I nearly fell off the chair laughing, but it taught me to always tell the kids when I was joking, and I did apologize to the class.

As I got older, I grew to love the questions that came from children's mouths.

My hair was getting gray, and one of the kids asked me if this was natural. "Well, I confess that every morning I take chalk and carefully apply it to each strand to make me look older. They were silent.

"Really", I said, "I am just teasing, I wish it wasn't turning gray, but I am just aging."

The children have a natural, and unquenchable desire to know that I am human, and it connects us together when they see that I am. All the schools in which I have taught give me the chance to show this human side.

While I was in Canton, I worked through some local schools and ministered to prisoners who needed help with their reading skills. One such prisoner has reinforced greatly my reasons for being a teacher and Sister.

His name is James. He left school early to help his family and fell in with the wrong crowd. One of 11 children in a home full of drug and alcohol abuse, the kids took to the streets to avoid the fights that went on at home between their mother and father. Some of these fights were so bad that his mother was seen chasing his father with knives or other weapons. His mother spent a great deal of her hard life in and out of mental institutions.

James was serving three years for the crime of breaking and entering. He and a buddy were looking for money for drugs and were caught, although James claims to be innocent.

When I first met James, he had the reading skills of a third grader. He was glad for the help I provided and we explored many varieties of reading. James was raised a Christian, and we often discussed religion at great length.

After attending drug rehabilitation, and improving his proficiency in reading, James was able to face the world outside of prison. His education stopped at the prison gates, but he did learn something while he was there.

Every once in a while, I hear from James. He is doing

very well. He got a job with an oil company and now lives with friends in rural Mississippi. The friends run a cafe and James help out when he is not working at the oil company. He runs errands, cleans, and helps around the business.

When he contacts me it is to thank me for the help, and for sticking with him inspite of his place in life. He appreciates knowing that he is accepted unconditionally by me. The last call from James was at 4:30 in the morning. He left a message on my answering machine telling me that he was thinking of me, and letting me know how thankful he was to be out of prison and surviving happily.

It is only through these missions with James and others that I am able to truly appreciate the gifts that have been given to me. Truly God is a steady presence to all of his people.

I love all the children here in New Orleans. I feel that my classes should be fun and informative for them. When we share our lives with each other, we learn to accept and love all God's children.

I love sports, and when we have contests with jump-roping the children love to cheer me on, and watch me compete. "You go girl!" I love their zest.

We go to haunted houses together, and scream together, and every Monday we discuss our week-end activities. The children share their stories, and I share mine.

When I was at a retreat years ago, the Sisters and I would greet each other with a bow and say a Latin phrase that meant, "I honor the God in you, as I honor the God in me." I have carried this tradition to the classroom and each day we bow to each other and say these words.

These moments allow us to start each day and each week embracing God's energy. Using this phrase allows us to see the small miracles in each day. Children are so open to accepting spirituality and I am blessed to be in a position to share it with them.

My current work is in East New Orleans. We, 13 total Sisters here now, work at a nearby school where not everyone wants to teach because of the neighborhood, so they are always badly in need of Catholic teachers. We live in some low income housing for elderly citizens in the area. Every day I am reminded how much I have to learn and how much our presence really means to the people here.

For example, there is always a threat of some crime, but we have a guard at the housing building and we are a faith-filled group. About a year ago, my car and another woman's car were scratched in the parking lot by vandals. She commiserated with me and suggested that we pray together and pray for the soul who damaged the cars. This is the kind of faith that surrounds me here. They have so little materially, and yet so much faith and they are so open about prayer.

Recently, my bike, which I keep locked at the bottom of the staircase, had both tires punctured. (Probably a group of youngsters visiting their grandmother were fooling around.) I took the bike to the local bike repair shop to have the tires fixed.

Again, the women that I live with were sympathetic, and helpful. When I went in to pay the bill and pick up my bike, the gentleman in the shop said, "this bill has been taken care of." What a surprise, it was so wonderful. I truly believe that greater good comes out of any evil. Each day I am blessed with the eyes to see our purpose and how much our presence means to this community, and I am humbled by their faith.

*Sister Bonita Brand taught school for 31 years. She start-
ed teaching in 1945, and continued working with Catholic
Schools until she retired about 4 years ago. Today she
manages a building where retired persons live in the city
of Chicago.*

-N.B.

Around 1950, I was teaching in Sioux City, Iowa.
Michael came to my fourth grade class with a very
visible chip on his shoulder. His terrible temper
and moods left no room for smiles, and he was disruptive
and unfair to the other children in the class. I felt his greatest need was friends, yet, friends are hard to come by when
one has such a temperament.

I arranged a project whereby the students were to write a
letter to a fellow student, mentioning pleasing characteris-
tics that person had. The letters would be unsigned and all
were urged to only say nice things.

Writing with a child's script, I wrote to Michael what I
knew he needed to hear. Positive things about his gregari-
ous nature, sense of humor, and cool way he dressed were
the main points that I wrote about. On opening his envelope, Michael shot up in his seat, smiled as I had never seen
him smile before, and looked around at the class to see who
could have sent him the letter.

His smile became permanent, and since he did not know
who his admirer was, he was Mr. Good Guy to everyone!

This took place in early fall. Just before Christmas
Michael became ill and died of intestinal complications.
The hospital conducted an autopsy which showed that he
had been born with a twisted intestine that finally wore thin
and caused his death.

It was such a tragedy. At the funeral his mother told me that he would 'have climbed mountains' for his classmates!

I thanked God for giving Michael two months to be the happy boy God had created him to be.

In the 1960's I was teaching in St. Mary's school in South Chicago. The classes were merged into double grades, which sometimes caused a problem if there were multiple family members in one classroom. This was the case with Jeanine.

Jeanine was technically in first grade, and her sister was in second. There was another sister not far behind who would be entering school in another year. Jeanine was a timid, nervous first grader and was completely overshadowed by her older sister who was outgoing, and quite smart.

As a rule, we teachers try to avoid retention (holding a child back a grade) because it can be regarded as a shame on the entire family. In Jeanine's case I really felt that another year would allow Jeanine the chance to have a better foundation in reading and mathematics and allow her to develop her personality.

I presented my arguments to Jeanine's mother and she finally agreed to talk to Jeanine about 'staying back'. They both agreed.

Allowing that two years between the sisters was the key to Jeanine's spirit. The next year she was the head of her class. School, which had been such a trial, was now a joy! Nervous mannerisms disappeared and were replaced by a happy little girl who bounced around in my classroom. Jeanine had experienced NEW LIFE! In return those around her experienced new life too.

Sister Eileen Geimer has been a teacher in inner city Catholic Schools since 1965, teaching pre-school through fifth grade. Currently she is teaching Kindergarten at Children of Peace School in Chicago. Sister Eileen said that she has never been nervous teaching in the inner cities, that she has only found people filled with goodness, desirous of a good education.

-N.B.

C hildren are constant sources of surprise, wisdom and humor. There have been many times when I have had to use all my self-control not to burst out with giant peals of laughter at some of the responses I receive from them.

I was teaching fourth grade at East Side Vicariate in Detroit and trying to go through groups of things with the children. "There are gaggles of geese, herds of cattle, flocks of birds..."

No one seemed to be responding to this line of discussion, so I asked, "Does anyone know what you call a group of people who cross the desert?"

Anna, a particularly precocious student, was ready to burst from her seat raising her hand madly, and carrying an eager expression on her face.

"Yes, Anna?" I asked.

"Globe-trotters," she replied proudly.

When I was at St. Gregory's on the north side of Chicago, there was a father of one of my students who told me a very funny story about his 5-year-old daughter.

The evening before Samantha began kindergarten, her father sat her down to explain how things would change now that she was going to school.

"You will have to go to bed earlier now," he explained, "because you will be getting up earlier. Everyday from now on the schedule will be like this, because school will be every day."

Samantha, turned on her heel, tossed her head and said, "Well, Toto, I guess we're not in Kansas anymore."

One of my favorite memories of teaching was one particular class who taught me to look at celebrations in a whole new way. The kindergarten class was practicing for a spring pageant. The song we were doing was "Do Re Mi" and I told the class that no matter what happened during our performance, they should all just keep on singing.

I asked the class, "Do you know why you should all just keep singing?"

One little child answered, "Because people might be shouting: Bravo! Bravo!"

Another one piped in, "Because they might be throwing us roses!"

Some weeks later in religion class I was telling all of the children how good God was to us. It was as if they all had an epiphany! They all threw their hands up as if they were throwing flowers to God and they yelled, "Roses, roses!"

I have no idea how many roses of delight we tossed during that school year, but I do hope that whenever those children experience the goodness of God during their lifetime, they will keep on throwing roses!

Listening and Hope

Sister Carmen Coccimiglio taught grade school and high school for 24 years in Detroit, Michigan. She taught business subjects after receiving her Masters in Business Education and then went on to earn her Masters in Theological Studies which prepared her for her current work at St. Vincent dePaul Church in the inner city of Pontiac, Michigan. For the past 10 years she has served as the Pastoral Associate at St Vincent dePaul.

-N.B.

One of our Living Word practices is to listen in contemplative silence and this is difficult to do. Often when I come to prayer, there is the tendency to rattle off numerous requests - so many needs of those to whom I minister, so many of my own needs, and yet, it is only when I stop talking that any response can be heard from above.

My best preparation for any appointments is to spend some time in quiet prayer, asking the Lord to be present through me to whomever I am meeting and whatever lays ahead.

This was the case with Rhoda. She came to see me because she had a deep secret that was aching to come to the surface. This well kept secret was not only causing her agony and unrest, but also affected her loved ones.

She was a newly married woman who was wrestling with the idea of sharing her deep secret with her new husband. It was with great agony and through tears and heaving sobs, that Rhoda confessed that she had been molested at a very early age. She had never told anyone because she felt that she had done something wrong and was being punished.

What does one do when faced with such a situation? Be present...all I could do was be the presence that she needed. I listened and held her as she sobbed for quite a while. When the opportunity came, I affirmed her, by helping her to realize that she was not at fault and needed not to seek forgiveness, but to seek strength from the Lord to reveal this hurt to her new husband. We prayed together for her and for the one who violated her. We prayed that she would have the strength to go on with her life and to share this secret with her spouse.

After a time, I saw Rhoda and her husband at Mass together. They saw me and looked at each other, and then came to me and embraced me. They did not have to speak for me to know that revealing her secret was the key for this couple.

By using this gift of contemplative silence, my soul is opened and available to the wisdom from above. Sometimes my call is just to be present to someone in need, to listen, to weep with them, and to pray for them.

I arrived where I am today through the Spirit guiding me. I taught in grade schools for 24 years before I moved on from my Masters in Business Education to my Masters in Theological Studies. I had always been a teacher. I started teaching grade schools, then high school, and finally business classes in high school after I received my M.A. in Business Education.

It was while I was working at an inner city school in Detroit that I was led to seek a position in church ministry and work towards my Masters Degree in Theological studies.

In my spare time, while teaching, I was asked by the parish to help set up a religious education program in the church. I found that my work with this program was extremely enriching. When I was called to work with a church in Pontiac, Michigan in 1988, I was eager to undertake the work.

Our church, in the inner city, has about 700 families, mostly Hispanic, who come to us because we welcome them all unconditionally. Some churches give strangers new to their flock tasks to do before they are accepted into programs, but, we find, that by opening our arms to all we have a strong parish, full of great faith.

I never cease to be amazed at the help that is needed by this community, and by the help that is provided by the same. It seems miraculous that whatever goes out the front door, comes in the back. I have seen this with my own eyes in the form of the Christmas boxes that the parish supplies for those in need, and to the requests for aid that are filled.

My ministry allows me to be present for engaged couples, those in troubled marriages, those seeking communion with the Church, the bereaved, those returning to sacraments, and those who need to confess or clear their troubled minds.

There are days when I am exhausted physically, and yet so fulfilled spiritually. I am truly blessed for the work that God enables me to do.

Those who are cradle Catholics perform our gestures and rituals without thinking. For myself, being a part of the Rite of Christian Initiation for Adults (R.C.I.A.), allows me to reconnect with those rituals, and acquire a deeper appreciation for the richness of the rites. Sometimes I am surprised by the participants in this faith journey. A couple of these surprises stand out in my mind.

It is customary that the parents of the children who are to make their First Communion attend five meetings. These meetings explain the contents of the text with which children are being presented. In this way the parents are able to supplement what the children are learning from the catechist. In addition, the program promotes parental participation in the religious education of their children.

The parent meeting is part of my responsibility and I enjoy this. This was the fourth meeting with these parents and the topic was the sacrament of reconciliation. I marvel at them, these parents. They have spent a long hard day at work and then come to sit for an hour to learn about religion. I try to make it worth their while and give them interesting information.

In this case, they learned about the history of the confessional. I stressed that the confession is a sacrament of peace. It is not easy to go to a priest and admit sinfulness, but it is worth the effort because, instead of feeling shame, we can understand our need for help and change.

Once the session was over and the parents were on their way, one of the mothers came over to me and asked when confessions were heard. Could she make an appointment to go to confession...adding that the last time she did this she was approximately twelve years of age. She seemed relieved to learn how circumstances have changed to make this sacrament more welcoming.

As we were talking, her husband came along and she responded to his appearance by stating that this year they were going to celebrate their tenth anniversary. Oh yes, what would it take to get married in the church?

Both are Catholic and at the time of their marriage, circumstances led them to a civil marriage and now they wanted to 'make things right'. What a grace!

Sometimes these are the surprises I get from time to

time. What I said or how I said it somehow led to the movement of the spirit within these parents. What a privilege to be an instrument through which the Spirit works.

There was a woman who came to me for advice on how to escape a bad marriage. Her husband was abusive and demanding. He refused to acknowledge her feelings or her ability to function as an adult, especially not as an equal.

She came for help because, after she sought and received a divorce from the courts, her husband still said that he had legal claims to her. He did not believe in divorce, and he felt that since they were married in the church, they were still legally married until the church said they were not.

I guided her through the annulment process, which sometimes seems complicated, and helped her come to terms with the loss of her marriage.

Finally, she was free. Free from the marriage, both civilly, and by the church. She felt she could now go on with her new life. She has been most thankful for the help that I was able to provide. For this I too was thankful.

It seemed like a simple thing to do, to guide her through a painful period. The church and its 'agents' do recognize suffering and we do have processes for changing bad situations. We both came through stronger by the grace of God.

Wholeness and Unity

*Sister Rosaria Schlecter teaches sixth grade at St. Marks
School in St. Paul, Minnesota. She has been teaching
there for 18 years. The primary reason that Sister Rosaria
came to Minnesota was that her mother was aging and she
wanted to be close enough to be able to help her mother
if needed.*

-N.B.

Sometimes it is hard to gauge how you are impacting
your students, especially the sixth graders. One day I
received this letter from a parent that really touched
me:

'Dear Sister, I am sure that from time to time you must
wonder if you are really reaching our children with Christ's
message. Well, something happened Friday night that I saw
as a demonstration of your ability to reach our young people and make a real difference in how they live their lives.

'On Friday night Tully, Jim, Joe, Josh, David, and Greg
won the 'lip sync' contest at the big dance. Tully slept at
our house and when he and Fred arrived home they were so
excited. They told me about winning the contest and then
they added that they were going to give the $10 prize to the
Rice Bowl at school (the Rice bowl is an annual Lenten collection for the hungry). I wish you could have seen their
faces when they said, "We're all going in together to give it
to Sister Rosaria." I saw so much love and anticipation of
the pleasure with which you would reward them. These six
boys had come up with this idea all on their own. You have
truly touched their lives with Christ's message. They even
went so far, when I suggested putting their good example in

69

the "Weekender," to say, "no, no! Then it wouldn't count."

I do remember clearly those boys bringing the money to me. It gave me such joy and hope to see how good these boys felt about doing such a generous thing. I was so proud of them. These are very hard times for kids because there are so many choices for them. Yet, in these young adults I see concern, generosity and spirit.

Sometimes, one's impact on students is not obvious for many years. This was the case with Jim. I taught him in sixth grade about seven or eight years ago. Recently, I received a note and an article from his mother.

Jim had become a writer for his college newspaper. He wrote an article telling about how he had gone to a bank before his Thanksgiving break, only to encounter a robbery and subsequent investigation. The article described how Jim had not even realized there was a robbery until the bank manager grabbed his arm and directed him to the lobby where those present were asked to describe anyone they had noticed in the bank. Jim had barely noticed the dark figure next to him because he had been staring at the bank teller. He felt bad about describing the alleged suspect because he did not actually witness the robbery and the only man he had seen had been African American.

Jim explained in his article, "The suspect? I remember staring at the beautiful bank teller in front of me while this supposed robbery took place. So true to my Catholic upbringing, I tried to act as though I had no idea of who had done it. I suddenly returned to sixth grade and heard Sister Rosaria saying 'we are all God's children.'" (*The Daily Cardinal*, University of Wisconsin, Madison, Welcome issue 1997.)

The attached note from Jim's mother said, "I thought you

would enjoy this."

What was powerful for me, as Jim's former teacher, was the fact that he named me and used a very simple quote. The words came alive to Jim and in his mind he had felt that it would be wrong to describe the only man he had seen simply because he was a man of color. How wonderful that these words and memories were present in this former students life.

Some of the pleasures that I receive from the students come unexpectedly. Such was the case with a note that I received from one of my students. This girl was one of several students who loved to give me a hard time about religion and teaching. She wrote me the following note at the end of the school year.

'Dear Sister Rosaria, You are the one who teaches every day with kindness. You have made this year excellent and religiously fun-filled. I enjoyed the exercises most. You have stayed a great teacher throughout the school year even when people like me haven't been very nice. Stay the way you are and you will go fun places. Have fun with Sisters of the Living Word this summer. See ya next year. Your former student, Deidre. P.S. I will always remember the words on the bulletin board- "God is always with me I trust in the Lord."

It was particularly encouraging to know that the bulletin board had made an impression.

*Sister Barbara answered her call to Sisterhood in 1960.
She has been teaching for 25 years. Mostly she taught in
Catholic High Schools. After she earned her Masters
Degree in Reading she taught remedial reading. Her
teaching has taken her from Chicago to New Orleans. She
served on the Leadership Team for the Sisters of the Living
Word and now she is teaching continuing education
through Harper College in the suburbs of Chicago.*
-N.B.

In our arrogant youth there are many times when we need to be put in our place. I learned a wonderful lesson when I was a young teacher that I carry with me still.

I normally taught in a large classroom of 48-50 students, so when the opportunity came along to substitute for a teacher who only had 4 children, albeit emotionally disturbed, I jumped at the chance. Think of the difference I could make with so few children?

There was a boy, Billy, in the class who's reputation was known around school. He had a very short attention span, and the teacher warned me that he would be very difficult to keep on a task.

When I was working with the class, I was surprised greatly when he not only paid attention to me, but seemed to really be listening for about 10 minutes.

I finished the lesson, and commented to Billy, "Wow, you are really doing a great job paying attention."

'I must be a wonderful teacher,' I thought to myself. 'Maybe I just needed less children.

Then Billy spoke. "Do you know what?"

"What?" I queried.

"You look just like Julie Andrews."

It was all I could do to hold back my laughter. Here I was thinking that I was really connecting to this boy.

This story has come back to me so many times in my years of teaching. I found that when I think children are listening, there are so many more 'Julie Andrews' moments than those of profound connection. I use this illustration often to let other teachers understand their place in the teaching relationship.

Teaching is so much more than just relating information by rote. The teacher is simultaneously dramatic actor, historian and most importantly an example.

There are times when I wonder who is ministering to whom in this work. I have learned so much from the people that I have taught and served. There are times when I truly question who is learning more, them or I? One case in particular really stands out.

Several years ago I was teaching sophomores. One morning before class started Joseph appeared at the classroom door. My classroom was in an out-of-the-way place, so he really had to make an effort to come to see me. He was this 15-year-old person with tears beginning in his eyes. After a greeting, he came to the point.

"Sister, How do I make friends?"

I could empathize with Joseph. His parents were older than most of the other children, and his sister was deaf, so often the family communicated with touch, which was unusual for a 5-year-old boy. The other students found him to be 'different' and he was the object of a lot of teasing for his mannerisms.

We talked a little. I gave him a few hints and as I recall he really did try to make some changes. I recall that by his Junior and Senior years he had fewer problems.

The exchange led me to reflect on the importance of friends and the patience to nurture my own friendships. I think this student has made me be a friend to people that I might at first have written off. He helped me grow in my ability to appreciate those who grace my life with theirs.

Last year Sister Helen came to live in our building. She moved to us after 20 years of living in Iowa. This was particularly difficult for her because she was in the early stages of Alzheimer's. She knew that she needed to make the change, but it was still an emotional time.

Every day the Sisters and I drove Helen from her new home in Des Plaines to the Center in Arlington Heights. As it was the Christmas season, people were beginning to put out their lights and in the evenings, when we drove home, we would admire the lights.

What Helen did not realize, and what the Sisters who drove and myself came to appreciate, was Helen's delight in the lights. Each day we drove the same route, and each day was like a new revelation to Helen. It was as if God had put those lights there simply to delight her.

Helen is the kind of person who was always a delight to be around. She was always someone who could laugh at herself. She truly believed that whatever God gives you, there is something good that will come out of the exchange. Helen sees the gentleness in life, and this view has only been extended and reinforced as her disease has advanced.

This year, we picked Helen up at the nursing home where she is residing and took her out to see the lights again. I am not sure who enjoys the event more. Helen sees everything with new eyes. On the dark night as we edged our way along the explanations of joy are a revelation for me. Helen is indeed a gift to be around.

It seems so right to spend time enjoying the season with Helen. Just as the light of the Lord came into being on Christmas so many years ago, Helen seems to recreate that light for those of us who are blessed to have the opportunity to spend the time with her.

Harmony with Earth

Sister Colette Fahrner has worked in a variety of ministries over the years, including teaching and administration. Her specialty is pastoral work and religious education. She also served on the Leadership Team for the Sisters of the Living Word before she came to where she now resides at the Resurrection Retreat Center in Woodstock, Illinois. Her work in the Appalachian Mountains was extremely challenging. She worked with many people who lived below the poverty level, teaching them literacy. Life in the Appalachians where resources are limited and working with the Glenmary Priests and Sisters, who were environmentally conscious, taught her to appreciate the limits of our natural resources. She includes this appreciation in her new work.

-N.B.

God does provide, but in God's time and manner. In 1979 I was the director of religious education in a Chicago suburban parish and I began to feel the stirrings of a missionary call. My request to do missionary work in Appalachia was a new direction for our small and young religious community. I was asked to 'wait a while' and to help out the community by finishing off another Sister's commitment in a rural area school. In agreeing to do this I turned down what I considered a dream job in Nashville.

After two years I began to follow my call and worked as an Outreach Minister in Kentucky. At the end of the sixth year I was contacted by phone and offered the very same job in Nashville that eight years earlier I had let go. The person who called to offer the job, did not know that I had turned down the same job years earlier. You can imagine my surprise and great delight.

In retrospect, I realized that there were important things to be done with the other parish, and lessons that I needed to learn before I would be ready to tackle the job in Nashville.

I worked in the Appalachian Mountains in the Outreach program through the Glenmary Sisters and Priests, teaching literacy to the impoverished. The thrill of this work, which progressed slowly, was the amazing transformation of an adult from someone who could not read to someone who saw life with new eyes.

The most difficult thing about teaching adult literacy is catching the students at the right moment in their lives. Generally, this time was when their youngest child was off to school, or when their children were grown and moving onto a new phase in their lives.

There was one woman whom I was teaching who was so excited about learning to read. She was recommended to me through a home nurse who knew that this woman was isolated. I remember her joy at each new step in the learning process, the first sentence she could read, the first sentence she could write.

There was a man who was so excited when he read his first road sign, and his family shared in his joy.

The work in Kentucky was very rewarding spiritually, but exhausting physically. When I left Kentucky, I was ready to seek new avenues of discovery. There were lessons left to learn and new worlds to left to discover.

My work in the Appalachian Mountains in Kentucky put

me in touch with the environment and allowed me to learn a great deal about appreciating our natural resources. It is easy to forget the importance of nature when one spends so much time indoors or in cities that seem to have forgotten what an old tree can contribute to a community.

Where we were located, water was a scarce resource and we were very conscientious about conserving it. If we did not, we would run out of water and have to wait for the wells to refill, which could take days. The Glenmarians were also involved in protecting the land from strip-mining and destruction from modern developments.

From this teaching I came to really appreciate the natural world. I developed an appreciation for gardening and landscaping, and for understanding the four elements and how we can incorporate them into our daily lives.

My new work as Creation Spirituality coordinator at a retreat in Woodstock allows me to combine this appreciation for nature with my current work. The retreat has 86 acres of woodlands and prairie that are partly being restored.

One project, in which we included the children was to have them each go outside and claim a small corner of the yard that they found attractive. They were to study why it was attractive, be aware of it, describe it, name it, and spend some time with it. The girls really took to this project. They dotted the lawn like polka-dots and were really connecting to the meaning of the project.

This connection to nature and to God's world is a key part of understanding how the elements work in our sacraments. In the rituals that we practice we incorporate the flame, water, the earth, and the air and yet many are unaware of this when witnessing the same rituals again and again in their daily lives.

Once aware of this connection, the mind awakens to the beauty of the ritual and how establishing this relationship with nature brings us all the closer to God. This connection is as natural as breathing, and I am blessed to have it be such a strong part of my life.

There never seem to be enough natural surprises for me. I like to approach each day as a connection with nature. One of the ways that I make myself connect with the day is to see each day for the air. When I go outside, I study the air and its elements. There are days when the air is crisp and cold, or heavy with humidity. The wind can be strong and moving, or quiet and soothing. Each day seems to have its own personality.

One breezy day, on a walk last autumn, I entered the woodland as I always do, following the paths that wind through the quiet. As I examined leaves and tracks left behind in the changing seasons I came upon a raccoon who appeared to be exiting a log. At first, I was startled to encounter such a wild creature unexpectedly, and then I realized that he was recently dead.

The strange thing about the raccoon was that he was standing stiff legged as if he were walking forward. He had literally stopped in his tracks. He looked stuffed. His lifeless eyes were gazing into space, and I raced back to the center to bring the students to see him.

To the students, the raccoon was an unexpected religion lesson. We speculated on why the raccoon died, and how. We examined this beautiful creature up close and safely. It was a wonderful lesson in the way that God works in the natural world. There in the silence and purity of the woods the kids were able to experience a graced moment. This was a lesson that would not soon be forgotten by the students that day.

Yes, nature's constant changing never ceases to inspire and amaze me.

Reverence for Earth's Gifts

Sister Laurita Saunders taught for 42 years in schools around the Chicago area. Her favorite subject was mathematics, and while she claims to have been tough as a teacher, the fondness of her students is evidenced by how many have kept in touch with her, invited her to reunions and been moved to enter into ministries. Today, and for the last 12 years, Sister Laurita, has worked on fundraising development for the SLW. These stories are from her time as a teacher and as a fundraiser.

-N.B.

I loved teaching. I tried to make school as fun and challenging as I could for all the students, and I also tried to introduce them to things they would not normally have experienced. I have always believed that if you want to really do something you sometimes have to be creative to get it done.

I was teaching in Wheeling and decided that taking a class to Washington D.C. would be a good way to have a hands-on history lesson. The problem we encountered was that, in order to rent the bus for the trip, we needed to have more people than the 10 students we had in the class.

So...we invited all the parents and even other relatives to come along. It was a trip to remember. The parents, I suspect, had just as much fun as the kids, and the students kept commenting on how they had never seen their parents so relaxed and frequently silly. Everyone was educated on this trip.

I am not a musician. In fact, I have a hard time carrying a tune, but, I decided that we needed chorus at our school to put on programs for the parents. To help, I enlisted the expertise of the boys from another nearby school.

These kids were fabulous. They directed the whole program, ran rehearsals, and carried off many great shows. The benefit for them was the experience and confidence they gained.

For the kids I was teaching the benefits were that we got a chorus, which taught them basic music, and sounded pretty good. Best of all, they did not ever have to hear me sing.

One of the schools that I taught in had many students from affluent families. Their parents were frequently out of town, and they really did not take their children to many places, so I made it a point to give the kids experiences that would have lasting memories.

As a coincidence, I was a big fan of the Chicago Cubs, so we went to many games over the years. I knew that the kids really enjoyed this. When I retired, one of the girls just couldn't stop crying.

"Why are you so sad?" I asked.

"With you gone, I won't be able to go to any more fun places."

At a recent reunion, the class gave me a book about the Cubs to thank me for all the games and events we attended. It is nice to think that these memories had such an impact on these children, who are now adults. Many of my former students have gone on to accomplish great things. Some are community leaders, some have entered the priesthood, and so many have kept in touch over the years. I enjoy the opportunity to have watched them grow and to have been a part of that growth process.

⊰✤⊱

When we formed this community of Sisters, we were pretty lost on how we would find the funds to do our work and on how we would stay in touch with the people who would contribute to our community. I suggested that we have a dinner/dance for the people who helped and supported us so that we could connect with them, and let them know how we were doing and to enjoy a nice dinner.

We planned everything for weeks. Finally, the big night came, and we were all set up at the Starlight Inn by O'Hare airport near Chicago. I was in charge of the raffle, and we had put all of the tickets in a box before they were to go in the drum for the drawing.

When it came time to transfer the tickets, they were nowhere to be found. My heart started beating as we looked high and low for those tickets. I even drove back to the Living Word Center, thinking they had been left there, no tickets.

I was coming close to panic, and thoughts were racing through my head. What would everyone think? I have really let everyone down. What was I going to do? Where were the tickets? I enlisted the help of the hotel staff, we looked in garbage cans, in the kitchen, under the tables, everywhere, but no tickets.

As I passed through the dining room, I barely noticed the dancers and diners. They were oblivious to me and my panic, and I was oblivious to them enjoying themselves. I grabbed a young man named Roger who had been helping us, and we drove once more back to the Center to look again.

As I was praying madly, "Please God, help us find those tickets, " I could hear Roger's voice in my ear.

Roger was calmly saying to me, "Take it easy Sister

Laurita, they will turn up. You are going to find them. Calm down, don't get yourself so upset. " (Remember I was probably, at 66, a really old woman to him.)

We still did not find the tickets. We returned to the restaurant, and decided on plan B. We would fill in slips of paper and have the drawing that way. Before we began writing madly, I asked the hotel manager to check one last time in the garbage. This time, he found them. Imagine my relief!

When I think back on that day, I remember my panic, and I remember Roger's calm voice. Roger hopes to enter Seminary after finishing college. He will make a good priest.

Her Song is Compassion

Sister Joanne Grib has a degree in Chemistry. She has been a nun for 47 years. She taught in various schools and in various positions for many years before she began working for a local Chemical Company in suburban Chicago. She worked in the Research Department for seven years and then came to work in the Computer division. Currently, Sister Joanne is working with her department on the conversion of computers to the new millennium designs. She came to be where she is because she felt that there was not enough religion in the marketplace. Every once in a while she asks God if she is doing the right thing, and invariably, she receives a sign to let her know that her work is vitally important. These stories are some of those signs.

-N.B.

There are many challenges that I face, being a nun and working in the marketplace, but I have found that my presence is sometimes all that is needed for many of the people that I work with.

For instance, there was a man that I work with who told his boss that he would not work with me under any circumstances. His words, which he later related to me, were, "I don't want no damn nun telling me how to run my life."

Recently he said that I was the greatest thing that ever came into his life. "Sister," he said, "You don't tell me how to run my life, you show me."

Another woman told me that I was responsible for her returning to the church. "You know Sister," she explained, "It is your fault that I went back to the church. Everyday, I look at you and I see how happy you are, and I said to myself, 'I want to be happy, too.' So I started going to church again, and you know, it worked."

People have come to me when they are troubled. One woman at work was notified that her husband was killed in a freak accident. Her co-workers came and brought me to her. We talked, and cried, and prayed. I did not know what to say, so I let the Holy Spirit do the talking. Some time later she wrote me a note telling me how much I had helped. Her friends told me that they hope I am still around if anything tragic happens to them.

There are others who ask me to dinner to talk about why they left the church, or they describe bad experiences that they had. One young couple had gone to their local parish to talk to a priest about marrying them, and counseling them. They could not find the door to the rectory, and instead ended up at the convent.

The nun they met chastised them, saying, "you two are too young to get married, go home and grow up." Needless to say, the couple was very discouraged about the church after that. They got married in the Village Hall.

When I met them, they decided that they wanted to make the marriage right. I helped them work with a local church and recently they renewed their vows.

Just when I think I do not belong here, someone in need comes to me and asks me to listen. Then, I am reminded that just being a gentle presence is important in the lives of my colleagues. What joy to feel so blessed.

About a year ago, Bill, one of the male employees, a young man of about 30 had a tragic experience in his life. His wife left him without any warning, taking with her their three daughters and one son. Bill was devastated by this and went into a terrible depression. One day he attempted suicide. He was taken to the hospital and was under psychiatric care for several months.

When he returned to work, I was asked by his immediate supervisor to 'keep an eye on him'. This was not too hard to do because I knew him fairly well and had worked closely with him in the past. Bill did not know that his boss had asked me to 'care' for him, and on his own, he asked me if we could meet at lunch time for a talk.

We met once or twice a week just to talk. On one occasion I mentioned to Bill that I thought it might be a wise idea to ask God for help because his problem was, as he described it, 'bigger than the both of us'. He agreed, and so we began praying together spontaneously at the end of each lunch.

Soon Bill was on his feet again and was back to being his old self with a few wonderful changes. He found a church to attend and now has become a regular church goer. His wife noticed the change in him too and after several more months of talks and discussions between them, returned with the children.

Bill and I still meet, but with less frequency and with many more laughs in our conversation. It is always wonderful to see the Lord working through someone to help restore their soul. It reminds me of the words, "Come to me all who labor and are heavy laden, and I will give you rest. Take my yoke upon you and learn from me; for I am gentle and lowly in heart, and you will find rest in your souls. For my yoke is easy, and my burden light." -Matthew 11: 28-30

Her Song is Love

*Sister Mary Cornille works at St. Ita Church in
the Edgewater neighborhood on Chicago's North side.
She has been the Pastoral Minister there for two and
one-half years. Prior to that she spent 30 years teaching
and administrating in various Chicago area Catholic
High Schools.*

-N.B.

It was late January, and the day prior to this day we had
determined among the administration that we could not
accept any more students. We had one of those schools
that never quite had any surplus money, and yet, always had
just enough. This day a girl came into my office and
implored me to accept her into the school.

Her story was remarkable. She was 15 or 16 years old,
lived in a basement apartment, within walking distance of
the school with her mother who was ill, and her sister who
was handicapped. They received disability income, but this
child worked 8 hours every night at a nearby restaurant in
order to help the family survive.

"I can pay my own tuition," she said with great pride, "I
can pay $25 per month." (The tuition at the time was about
$200 per month.)

I looked at her and various thoughts raced through my
head, "How can we possibly pay for one more student?
How can we provide proper education, or books, or elec-
tricity? I cannot take this girl's money. How could I possibly say no to this girl?"

I did accept the girl, and we refused to let her pay.

The very next day, I received a check in the mail from a
former teacher of the school. Inside the envelope was an

accompanying letter which read, "I have a wonderful new job this year, in a public school. I cannot help but think about all of you there at St. Gregory's. I make a good income and I want you to have this check to pay for the tuition of one girl who really needs it."

The Lord does work in mysterious ways.

My heart goes out to those in need around me. There are several who come to mind when I reflect on the people who pass me daily, enrich me greatly, and seem to appreciate my presence. Our parish has many poor elderly, immigrant, and mentally challenged persons.

One such woman could not afford to buy herself a hearing aid, and really missed hearing the things around her. I helped her fill out the forms and provide all the paperwork required to qualify for help through the Lions Club. When she came to her first Mass with her hearing aid, she was so happy and so thankful. Just seeing the light in her eyes was rewarding.

There is a man who is a veteran full of great spunk. He lost both his legs and spends a great deal of his time sitting in his wheelchair in front of the dismal 'nursing home' where he lives. He greets me each day with humor and eagerness, and every once in a while he brings me gifts. In his spare time he contacts radio stations having contests for tickets, or dinners, and when he wins he brings his winnings to me to share with another friend. His generosity, humor, and spunk, inspite of his disabilities inspire me to appreciate the blessings I have.

There is also Rosemary, a Nigerian woman who was earning her degree when she began to hear voices in her head. She tells me that she goes through a great deal of torment. Every once in a while she hears Jesus's voice, but the others torture her. I can only listen and share my heart with her.

Another man who comes to mind is the Mexican gentleman who works two jobs for his growing family, and could not find a home because he is Mexican. He can afford to pay the rent, but the neighborhood where he wanted to live would not rent to Mexicans. I tried to help him and finally he found his own place, where he pays more rent for less of a place. His daughter calls me Tia Maria, and I am honored to be part of his family. He is someone I listen to, help when I can, and admire for his hard work and his dedication to his family.

Finally, I think of the group of elderly women who we see regularly when we bring Eucharist to them in their retirement home. One of the women came to me one day, and said, "Sister Mary, you do not bring Jesus to me, Jesus comes to me and you just get to come along." How right she is.

Inspiring moments? I do not know if I have any real ones—big ones. Forever I have known that God loves me and lives in me. This thrill deepens a bit every day.

Often I get in the car to drive home at the end of the day and I pause in the quiet and feel the joy of being loved by God, knowing that Jesus came so that 'our joy may be full'.

I remember all the times of trying to do what Jesus said, and what the Sisters of the Living Word mission statement echoes, "the poor have the Good News spoken to them!"

I think of the struggling disadvantaged high school girl who came to talk about coming to our school, the man who tells me how he is refused renting because he is Mexican, the old lady who does not have enough money for a hearing aid, the legless veteran who sits in his wheelchair outside his dismal nursing 'home'.

I try to listen and to speak the Good News and love each one as the words of the Bible echo in my mind,

"I have come that you may have life and have it to the full", "The weak things of the world has the Lord chosen".

These are the words of Jesus and of the Sisters of the Living Word. How blessed I am to cling to both of them.

Editor's note

It was my great pleasure to interview the Sisters for these stories. I found each Sister to be gracious and modest about their achievements and very protective of the people that they have helped. In talking to them, I also found myself spilling my guts, sharing stories from my life, and generally being creative in my attempt to elicit one more story. I found that this sharing on my part allowed me to think of inspirational stories in my own life, like the following which would qualify under the heading of 'Harmony with the earth'.

This event happened last Spring. My sister and I were searching for arrowheads in my sister's cornfield. It was nearly sunset and we were trying to use the last few minutes of light in our hunt. There was a mist in the air, causing the sky to be a little darker than normal, and really we were heading back to the house, but too stubborn to give up the search yet. As we studied the earth on our way home, we heard a rush of air, and a honk of a Canadian goose close by. We turned, just as about 10 geese took off next to us.

The regal birds were so close that we had missed seeing them in the near dark. We could hear their wings, whoosh, whoosh, whoosh, as they lifted off from the barren field. We were spellbound. The sound was like no sound we had ever heard before, it was both peaceful and magical. It was a rush of air, so close we felt we could soar with those geese.

The birds were gone, just as quickly as they had appeared, and in their place was an amazing stillness. The mist shrouded the field and we felt such a strong connection to the earth, to each other, to God. We both looked at each other and knew that we had been given a gift. We smiled, gave up our search and headed back to the house with few words.

Sometimes, there is nothing to say. Sometimes God's voice is so loud, so full of beauty, that you are overwhelmed by the moment.

The following pages are for you, the reader, to document your own inspirational moments. Savor these moments. Share them with your children. They chronicle the times when you are closest to God.

Journal Pages

Index to the Sisters

Betty Betzweiser..19
Bonita Brand 59

Carmen Coccimiglio..63
Annamarie Cook...51
Mary Cornille 89

Jeannette Daniel...47
Judiann Derhake...45

Colette Fahrner...77
Joanne Fedewa...37

Eileen Geimer..61
Marlene Geimer..29
Joanne Grib...85

Phoebe Marshall...43
Barbara Mass...73

Mary Nicholas...53

Jeannine Randolph..23

Laurita Saunders...81
Rosaria Schlecter..69

Kris Vorenkamp..9

Mary Ann Zrust..33

For more information on the Sisters of the Living Word and their many missions, write or contact the Sisters at:

Sisters of the Living Word
800 North Fernandez Avenue B
Arlington Heights, IL 60004-5316

ph:(847)577-5972
fax:(847)577-5980
e-mail address: slw@slw.org
website: www.slw.org

The Save-A-Barn Small Press is dedicated to publishing creative works that raise the consciousness of those who read them.